The Other Mountain

Rowan Williams was born in Swansea in 1950. He was the 104th Archbishop of Canterbury (2002–2012). He spent much of his earlier career as an academic at the Universities of Cambridge and Oxford successively. Williams stood down as Archbishop of Canterbury on 31 December 2012 and became Master of Magdalene College, Cambridge, in January 2013.

Also by Rowan Williams from Carcanet Press

The Poems of Rowan Williams

ROWAN WILLIAMS

The Other Mountain

CARCANET

First published in Great Britain in 2014 by
Carcanet Press Limited
Alliance House
Cross Street
Manchester M2 7AQ

www.carcanet.co.uk

A CIP catalogue record for this book is available from the British Library

ISBN 978 1 84777 449 1

The publisher acknowledges financial assistance from Arts Council England

Typeset by XL Publishing Services, Exmouth
Printed and bound in England by SRP Ltd, Exeter

Contents

Waldo Williams: Two Poems translated from the Welsh

For Patrick and Helen Thomas

Preface

The landscape of South and West Wales is a strong presence in many of these poems, and I want to acknowledge all those who have in different ways helped to shape the inner landscape that goes with that particular outer one. A long engagement with the work of Waldo Williams, teacher, Quaker, peace activist and – by common consent – one of the lastingly significant cultural figures of twentieth-century Wales, is evident in the translations of two of his well-known pieces, in the 'Carn Ingli' sequence, and elsewhere, as in 'Nagasaki' and 'Shell Casing', less explicitly. Waldo imagined his own work as a form of quiet but unyielding resistance to a hectic inarticulate violence in the mind, the fever-ishness that overflows in personal aggression as in wars and pogroms of all kinds. The centenary of the outbreak of the First World War – with little sign of fever abating – is a good time to remember him and to think about how poetry resists.

There are other tribute pieces here, for Dylan Thomas on the centenary of his birth, and Joseph Brodsky, as well as for the great Jewish artist Josef Herman, whose flight from European fascism brought him eventually and rather implausibly to a Swansea valley village in mid-century – the village of my own birth and early years – where he is still remembered with affection. And the theme of twentieth-century atrocity is also confronted in 'Yellow Star', celebrating the memory of the Russian nun Maria Skobtsova (recently declared a saint by her church), whose work for Jewish refugees in Paris in the 1940s led to her arrest and death in Ravensbrück concentration camp. Her declaration that all Christians should wear the yellow star that Jews were forced to wear by the Reich administration was an expression of her will-ingness to risk her life in solidarity; but it presents the question of what happens to that solidarity in a history of Christian flight from such identification – and worse. Still in mid-century, 'Nagasaki' was prompted by the story of Takashi Nagai, a profes-sional radiologist at the University Hospital in Nagasaki at the time of the bombing in which his wife Midori was killed; already suffering from radiation-induced leukaemia, he spent his later years both exploring the effects of atomic radiation and passion-ately advocating disarmament. In the background is the history of

Japanese Catholicism (in which the city of Nagasaki is very significant); and the ministry of Pedro Arrupe, later head of the Jesuit order, in the hospital at Hiroshima at the same time.

Other landscapes – Istanbul, rural Congo and more domestic ones – are visited here. The Cambridge sequence was commissioned as the text of a cantata, the music by Christopher Brown, performed to mark the anniversary of the University's foundation. Other commissioned pieces include 'Please Close this Door', written for the National Churches Trust and read by Geraldine James at a service to mark their sixtieth anniversary in November 2013; 'Arabic Class', written for a literacy campaign, 'Passion Plays', written for a special edition of the *Today* programme on Radio 4 edited by the singer and songwriter P.J. Harvey, and 'Host Organism' for a campaign on organ donation. My thanks to all who prompted these for their confidence and encouragement.

'Stations of the Gospel' attempts to find one compressed image for each chapter of St John's Gospel, one perception that could be captured in (roughly) a haiku form. 'Felicity' looks back to the record of a North African slave girl martyred for her Christian belief along with her mistress, Perpetua, in 203; Perpetua's own prison journal survives, and I suppose this poem asks what kind of 'prison journal' Felicity might have composed, deprived as she was of the status and literacy of her mistress and her mistress's friends, but still made to be a speaker, a subject, by the very fact of her extraordinary and terrible situation. Once again, the question is to do with what words resist butchery; what has to be said if manic violence is not the last word.

Rowan Williams

Acknowledgements

Some of these poems have appeared in the *Guardian*, *New Statesman*, *PN Review*, *Poetry Ireland*, *Scintilla* and *Theology*. 'Roadside/Viaticum' was written for a special edition of *Taliesin* (144, Winter 2011), the journal of the Welsh Academy, to mark fifty years of publication, and appeared in a Welsh translation by Alan Llwyd.

The Other Mountain

The Other Mountain: Riding Westward

March, sun and haze, five o'clock,
travelling west; and the cloudbank sets
firm ahead, another range of dove-grey
slopes, great waves suspended dangerously
over the nearer ridges, thrown up by some
grinding of plates on the sea bed and held,
tight as a bowstring in a photograph
of disaster just about to fall. The quiet mass
waits, the hill country without paths or stones
or grass, it drives down behind everything,
tucking its bulk into the mountain's back.
While dark melts into the spring haze,
the road draws nearer to that corner
where the hills meet; when the button
is pressed and the tape plays and the wave
falls, there is no path or stone
or grass, no root, no standing, the pale bodies
drift, lifting a hand to ask for leave
to speak, compassionate leave, always to be
compassionately refused.

From Carn Ingli

for Waldo Williams

1. Master Class

The children in the school yard run
to hold the old man's hand.

They hold the hand that ploughs,
like Dewi, stony soil.

Where words will settle, germinate,
build homes for fugitives,

For the lost children far beyond
the yard. He holds their hands,

He feels the silk folds, thinks
will his plough-hardened thumbs

Print on the silk the skill to carve
leaves for an open door? The children

Hold the engraved memorial hand,
lift faces for inspection,

Steer him into the school to meet
the other teachers for their gentle sentence.

2. Exit Tax

The Western shore is what the left eye sees,
where the headlands of the senses join up
into one frontier: I am a body, this
is an island. Furious or still, what sits
on the foreign side has no words in common.

Shores where day ends, light is pinched out,
where the hand feels in vain for a wall
not there and the foot misses the stair.
The West is where the dead sail; the blistered
slopes, the cloth-smooth pastures, the beds

Of the burns unit, waiting for the drop
into sleep and water. In the left eye's landscape,
some futures are not possible: the ones
where I rehearse the deaths of strangers,
where I sit back, president of a tribunal

Where all the questions have been silenced
and all the enemies are underfoot. The eye
of the headlands opens wide, and foreign
tongues from the neighbouring darkness sound
in curlew cries of mockery. Nothing is owed

To futures of terror. Better to write
on the cell walls a few green words
that the left eye can recognise. Good news:
the only tax you have to pay is death,
not fear, not insurance, not obedience.

3. A View

What is nightfall?
The two grey millstones meeting,
grinding the sweet furnace-bright berry, so that
the juice leaks out across the closing mouth.

What is daybreak?
Clay lips unsealed, a glimpse
down the long lane of moisture gathering
under the skin of the unconscious hours.

What is the shore?
The debris of an argument
between the level grammar of the sea
and the wild singular nouns of stone.

What is the word?
The swift, fired from a bowstring
buried in fern, against the padded walls
of quiet streaming upward from the hill.

What is the voice?
The single line as the hill crest swells,
the liquid brimming in its improbable meniscus,
on the edge, always, of dark streams falling.

What is pity?
Walking up into the colonnades of rain,
tasting the water and the running mucus as you grow
cold, knowing the skin is no defence.

What is peace?
Down in the nest of roots fumbling
for drink, a pouring without end
across the bruised dark sand.

4. Monument, Mynachlogddu

To shoe a troop of horse with felt:
stealing across the dry, resisting grass,
but not with mounted men, not

To break in to nightbound camps
and put surprised half-naked conscripts
back to sleep for ever, but

Beasts of a Quaker apocalypse,
with no authority to hurt, padding
and stopping on the soil that

Springs like a ballroom floor, soft and
dishevelled, keeping their sympathetic distance
from the stone's still eye.

Nevern Churchyard. The Bleeding Yew

Sliced clean as marble; a glassy mourner
bending to read the blunt letters, the routines
of leavetaking. But glass will splinter: ragged bites
stand open and the port-red ooze, crusted
like scale in kettles, wanders, slow as a winter fly,
across the arctic slope. Gashed bodies
push out their sickness through the skin:
the marble mourner has leached up the fevers
from the rubbed lives piled round its roots,
sucking the moisture of the leaf-choked, rust-throated
fountain forgotten in the wood, the well
of loss, wounds, endings, seeping out
under the prosaic stones, clouding the glass,
cracking the ice. The tree of discharge.

Caldey

The bay's mouth swells, sucking the gale
and spit into stone lungs, laying
the ground for what the island tells, hoarsely:
before the boats arrive, after the shops shut.

Beach

Sand shuffles amiably, like familiar words
stroking and nosing one another, melismatic
chant that slips and pours so quickly
that you never see the razor shell until
you feel grains rubbing the red flesh.

Coppice

Under the trees, the muttered conversations
of rain on leaves, wood, mast; dreams of pushing through
a restless crowd in this foreign town,
wondering what they suspect, what they fear,
what you look like to their glistening eyes.

Lighthouse

Bullets of water in the grey morning,
a lash of rapid pain on the cheek,
sparks from the boiling cloud, water
lifted, water dropped, something dissolving,
not an asperges; maybe, though, friendly fire.

Headland

Gulls cry their little sickle sounds
nicking the eardrums, scratching at the sea,
pecking and fishing into the confused sea light
inside, alert for the shine that tells them
where they can hook up something alive.

Breathing out, the long flare of late sun
runs to the horizon, the mouth says hoarsely:
you can tell how high the wind is
by how still the birds hang.

Herman in Ystradgynlais

The baked crust, humps, mounds,
streaked faces like the seams
bent sideways under the tread
of long hours; and it breaks
around the heavy shoulders, the surface
cracked for a second into white
liquid, a hot light beyond summer,
light from the steel-mill always
labouring under scorched soil
as the generations tread, tread,
into the dust, the gas, framed
for a second in liquid anger,
in a steel love the ovens cannot
dry. *Arbeit macht frei*? Not so; only
the labour of the hairline keyhole
surgery in the heaped dusk.

Swansea Bay: Dylan at 100

1.

A thumb drawn down, smearing the grey wash,
storm pillars float over a December morning,
the sun still tipping rocks with liquid
out at the headland. In the bay swells urge
this way and that; a dark patch swings
out from the sea wall, pushes the pushing current
sideways, the planes of water tilting by inches
under the lurid morning, heaving this way and that
beneath the mottled skin and pinching it into the long
blade of a wave, the knife under the cloth
ready to slice. Watching, you have no notion
how it all runs, the hidden weights swinging
and striking, passing their messages, hidden
as the pulses under the scalp, behind the eyes,
that sometimes pinch themselves into a sharp
fold, into an edge, as if the buried cranial dances
gathered themselves to cut, for a moment, at
the skull's dry case and break through in white curls.

2.

I sang in my chains. I listened for the pushing swell
of light in the country yards, the undertow
of bliss that still cuts at the cloth, at the bone,
at all the tired shrouds. I listened
for the tide retreating and the small lick and splash
of breeze on the trickles between corrugated sand,
for the silent footfall of pacing birds, processing
to their office. Beyond the bay, the infant-bearing sea
slips further off, the next room is quiet and the sun
whispers hoarsely. When I call in my dream for it,
my voice is small and the knife strains bluntly
at the knotted cloth. Watching the swell again
at whispering liquid sunrise, I have no answer
when I wonder how the world's sand runs
out of grace and the dark moods of the water
jostle each other; I cannot tell if they will gather
ever again, severing the milky web that holds me
mortally. Do not go. Now as I was

Cambridge at 800

1. Landscape

The river swings slowly on the clay;
a track in the cloud chamber, the old road
of Roman ghosts and lost dominion,
fingered with grass and mud, still carves the fen.
The little shrines of clunch and rubble sit,
shuttered against the needles of a draught
that treads the cloud chambers like a legion.
As if the first settler here was winter,
a slow craftsman of the shining wires
and filigrees, laying bright frost on black soil.

2. Divinity

Frost on black soil: when the first clerks,
wrapped tight, caps drawn down,
first intoned the dry music, blew on the sparks

And rolled from the furnace the glass spires,
twined close and polished hard,
the castle of the schools, they kindled other fires,

Slow-burning, flaring at last around the boards
of White Horse Tavern chambers,
as the restless Word scorched off its cords.

But the scrubbed reformed sky still yearns for motions,
deep vortices, storm towers,
for journeys into Plato's paradise, devotions

Like the draught's needles piercing the glass of sight,
stitching philosophy
into close music, into a formal velvet night

Of bowing constellations. Hung on the walls,
two centuries' worth of weaving,
the warm needlework of Greek that calls

The clerks to stir and dance again with the Word's
soundings, returnings,
filling the sky's towers, nesting and circling birds.

3. *Natural Philosophy*

Nesting and circling: vision catches
this or that landing place, guesses
this or that current down which to glide,
maps out the architecture
of stone and air alike.
The eye in flight, steadily as the river's
curved arm, traces a single horizon
behind the crenellations and the little shrines,
and a young Christ's man steps on board
for the long voyage to damp islands
where the forms heave out of water
inch by inch into defining light.
Back home the sculpting wind cuts deeper,
frost cracks down to the joint
of one and marrow at the heart
of matter, the split anatomy of power
flowering for life and death. Life's letters
are decoded, rescued from the floods
of blood and breathing, hung in dry waterfalls,
stuttering an episodic song, the marks
and pauses of an aboriginal art.

4. Humanities

Marks and pauses: where we cannot speak
we must not, where we can we must,
and watch for the dishonest leak

Of casual silence where the white drifts
would bury needful, spare, unsparing words
of scrutiny; or of casual talk into the rifts

Of emptiness that mirror the uncrowded sky.
Power tends to corrupt, the patriarch said,
casting a patient, unmerciful, Germanic eye

On the soft histories we love to tell
(as if our past were beautiful and frozen
in what we say, locked in the cell

Of our control). Even in the cold
marshland, there is the heat of protest:
this is a critic's landscape, shaped to hold

The black no less than the bright,
and the sharp stripped trees no less
than the water: night

Where the stars' little wounds drop streams
of slender clarity, no less than days of mist
and the mumbled theatre of waking dreams.

5. Townscape

Waking dreams: across the lakes
of glowing grass, the wedding-cake
pinnacles drape themselves with ice.
Into the nest of grass, timber,
Tudor brisk and stone, the straight
fen tracks run silently, treading
like a legion. Yellow-grey houses,
small clay ovens against winter,
stare at the postcard castles from time
to time: quizzical, grateful,
suspicious, knowing they are needed,
shrugging at the mind's obsessional
drive to forget where it belongs
and what it owes. And the Roman roads
fortify themselves in glowing glass
where the academy as it passes
reads silicon reflections. Roads, houses,
river, ice-framed sanctuaries,
all of them framing the human eye
discovering the human eye
within the human eye's fathomless black soil.

Door

Lift the stone and you will find me;
Split the wood and I am there
Gospel of Thomas

A book falling open, the sliced wood
peels apart, jolting for a moment
over the clenched swollen muscle:
so that, as the leaves fall flat
side by side, what we read is the two
ragged eyes each side of a mirror,
where the wrinkles stream off sideways,
trail down the cheeks, awash with tears,
mucus, mascara. *Split the wood*
and I am there, says the unfamiliar
Lord, there where the book opens
with the leaves nailed to the wall
and the silent knot resolved by surgery
into a mask gaping and staring, reading
and being read. Split the wood; jolt
loose the cramp, the tumour, let the makeup run,
the sap drain, the door swing in the draught.

Roadside / Viaticum

Blisters of rain on plastic wraps around
the flowers, the curling flowers with their life
peeling away steadily: *upon such sacrifices*
the incense is in short supply. Flowers
for a thankyou, for a last-minute birthday
present for your mum, for an embarrassed
girlfriend. Death, smiling and nodding, says,
It was no trouble, or, lips pursed, it's nice to see
how thoughtful you can be, or else just grins and blushes.

When you wake, crying, what you want
– failing your mummy – is your teddy. When
you go through the lethal crash barrier,
we cannot tell you when it will be morning
but we can give you memories of desperate
innocence to cling to. Death, always a soft touch,
says, Ah: sweet. I like it when you just get
used to it, savouring the tears in the sodden fur
and cloth. Saves you the trouble of getting up.

At the road's edge, we mouth like children,
blisters of water on our faces, lips
and limbs trembling. Left behind by the family car,
we wait under the rain, over the peeling flowers,
trying to remember why we mustn't
jump into cars with strangers. Come on, says death,
no point in standing in the wet. And you can stop
looking for more than fur and flowers, as if someone
were coming back for you from beyond the crossroads.

Stations of the Gospel

I

All music twisted in one string:
reach out with your long nail,
touch. Listen.

II

Poured from this stone, the water
stings, the mind lurches, suspects
joy, chaos.

III

The wind passes
no sentence: carries scent, sound,
a face felt in the dark.

IV

Thirst drops in the long
dark, swallowed cold by the eager
earth-streaked water.

V

In the deep pool
what fish is wandering through, to make
the dead limbs ripple?

VI

Bread's flavours: sand,
grass, salt, stone, blood, an open cut
from the shore's litter.

VII

Hands close on absence,
on broken waters from the cave
beneath the ribs' vault.

VIII

Before all journeys
there is the desert sky, glass-
clear, ice-resonant.

IX

Light catches the slicked
sand, ash, glances behind shut
eyes, opens a wound.

X

No no. Dusting away dazed
flies, he forces the lock;
snow blows in.

XI

Acid tears fall, corrode rocks
in foam, burn away
in shock the grave's knots.

XII

The bowl glows in the furnace.
Inside, the beads of sweat
spit and scatter.

XIII

On the worn shiny
boards the water runs, salt with
refuse from dark roads.

XIV

Door swings in the wind:
empty path, low sun ahead
blinds, slows steps, welcomes.

XV

Knifelike, the spring gales
peel skin from sour flesh shrinking
from the candid sun.

XVI

Long secret ends: blood-
smeared, a crown breaks the heaving
of the body's sea.

XVII

Stand here
before the mirror where you see
only the sun behind you.

XVIII

Splinters on paving
stone, red smears; through the window
foreign words stumbling.

XIX

Behind the soldiers' backs
the cloth tears slowly, soaked, eaten
with sour wine.

XX

Put your ear to the crusted gash
in stone or flesh; the mouth
speaks your name.

XXI

Catch it, catch it. The lake
brims over in the bright dawn,
runs from my hands.

Nagasaki: Midori's Rosary

The air is full of blurred words. Something
has changed in the war's weather. The children
(whose children will show me this) have been sent
to the country. In the radiology lab,
Takashi fiddles, listening to the ticking bomb
in his blood cells, thinks, once, piercingly,
of her hands and small mouth, knotting him in
to the long recital of silent lives
under the city's surface, the ripple of blurred Latin,
changing nothing in the weather of death and confession,
thinks once, in mid-morning, of a kitchen floor, flash-frozen.

When, in the starburst's centre,
the little black mouth opens, then clenches,
and the flaying wind smoothes down the grass
and prints its news black on bright blinding
walls, when it sucks back the milk
and breath and skin, and all the world's vowels
drown in flayed throats, the hard things,
bone and tooth, fuse into consonants of stone,
Midori's beads melt in a single mass
around the shadow with its blackened hands
carved with their little weeping lips.

Days earlier, in Hiroshima, in what was left
of the clinic chapel, little Don Pedro, turning
from the altar to say, *The Lord be with you,*
heard, suddenly, what he was about to claim,
seeing the black lips, the melted bones,
and so, he said, he stood, his small mouth
open, he never knew how long, his hands
out like a starburst, while the dialogue
of stony voiceless consonants ground across
the floor, like gravel in the wind, and the two
black mouths opened against each other,

Nobody knowing for a while
which one would swallow which.

To the City

1. Bosphorus

Once there were chains between the towers
shackling the green-black forest walls across the water
locked in each other's mirror-gaze, chains to choke off
the galleys headed greedily for the tense city. Not now:
this is a motorway shining with oil, the lanes
jostling and humming with their relaxed freight,
birthdays and anniversaries and conference excursions
bouncing and rocking along the cleft so confidently
you could forget the swimmers dead in the green-black
depths, the ones who failed to breach the walls
on the far shore or break the mirror. And the day trips
swing round and land where they began. But in the unquiet
morning dazzle, the dolphins arch and plunge, unannounced,
bright needles pulling threads between air
and sea. They stitch their trails round the lethal cruisers,
the crates of oil and spinning blades, come without call
or cause, go without mercy. Out of the green-black vaults
the thread leaps, wavering in unquiet light,
to tow the boats out of their channels, draw
shore to shore, face to face, swimmers to gulls and sailors.

2. Ayia Sofia

And that, the Greeks tell you, is the Conqueror's black handprint,
when he rode in over the ten-foot depth
of corpses; when he leaned over, pushing
the half-globe on its axis, swinging the arrow
towards a new, south-eastern, pole. The bars of light
lie angled silently, rolling against the tilted bell:
a tongue's thread cut. The foliage of immense
words painted curling and waving, unmown
green verges of a scoured field, drifts across open mouths
and scratched eyes, the layered dead
under the flaring frozen seraphs. There are no hours
to strike, no consecrating whisper to be marked, where death
so rolls and stacks its fields. Handprints of soot
inside the burnt domes of skulls; the empty segment
on the sundial, where worlds have pulled apart
and shadows stand unmoved, the clock's hands
are nailed still, the bell cracks open to a sky
of frozen stars pointed in accusation,
flaring on spikes, burning for the uncountable names
harvested by conquerors for this or that revelation's sake.

3. Phanar; the Patriarch's Cantor

Anastas. Leaning back, lifting elbows, braced,
jaw out, he curls fingers and lips, to make
his brassy diaphragm a bowl where the round gale
swings on itself, brushes the metal to a shine. Fingers
unfold into the quieter pulsing of a sandy breeze;
the drone shifts with a grind, brows are wiped,
a tired eight-year-old begins to cry, is hugged,
scolded, bundled behind the screen. The wind
starts rising once again, the couriers pick up speed
and ride into the gaping caves, the lifting wind
scrapes sandy flanks against the bowl of lung, sinus,
damp and bone. What does it carry, the straining
weight searing his arms against the stall's wood?
The creak of stones shifting on the hill; forests falling; a body,
massive, limp, released from its ropes around the mast,
struck dumb? The windy grains ringing half-audibly,
bouncing around the bowl's rim? He lifts
his palms again; welcomes the rising, the stone,
the grain, the body, the little pestle
drawn round the bronze. *Anastas.* Lifted.

Felicity

She is like a doll: not a doll
given by father, or an old doll
from your big sister. Like a doll
I gave things to get from a travelling man.
Blood is what I gave to get this one,
shouting in front of them, shaming us.
How will it be, they said, when the animals
come to eat you, how much will you
shout then? I say, I will be like
the doll then, I will be someone else's, bought
with the blood and noise of someone
else so I don't have to.

They bought me like a doll
from a travelling man, the man
who took me after they burned the town
when all the blood and shouting of my father
and my mother paid for me to live.
They bought me, a doll for a little girl
who is rich and pretty. Year after year
she plays with me. Her little brother
dies, his face eaten up like by animals;
her big brother puts his hands on me
to push me down and pour his stuff inside,
and I get ill and strange, the blood stops then starts again.

She is going to be married, the pretty girl. She is
not happy. She talks a lot. One night
I must go with her to a bath in the dark,
it is a secret, there is an old man
talking a lot, I will make you free,
he says, and puts his hands on me
to push me down (first I think no, no) and pours
and pours water like my brother would
when we were little by the pond, and I
feel like laughing: father, he says, son,
magic breath, now the old ladies
will give you new clothes. Her too,

She laughs and shivers, it is a secret,
it is not like the other secret when he comes
to push me down. There is a wedding,
then there is a little boy. Now says her brother
you would like one too, laughing, and pushes
harder and I get ill and strange again,
and the blood stops and I become fat; they say
bad words, but she holds me and shouts
at them, leave her alone, she is my sister.
Sister? Her father says, quite; sister,
like you have been together to the bath
in the dark, yes, she says, yes, do you want

Me not to call things by their right name?
that on the floor is a pot; she is
my sister. The he shouts and goes to hit her
and then he crumbles up and cries
and scratches his face and blood comes,
and he says, now they will come for you,
think of me and your brother and the little
boy. Her hand holds me tight and hurts
and hurts. Now she has no little boy
in here and I have my girl that I
bought with all that blood, and she tells
me dreams, how she climbs up

A ladder, every step between knives,
I think of climbing sharp strings,
like on a harp, and every step cuts
just at the moment when the note sounds.
And she dreams her little brother,
with his eaten face, so thirsty, but she prays
and his face comes clear and he puts it
into the pond and drinks and drinks, I think
of my brother in the sand by the pond,
cut all over, so thirsty and he cannot move,
and I think of the travelling men and wish
them thirst till they cannot speak.

And there are gardens, she says, old men
who smile and give handfuls of new cheese
and apples, and there is when she turns
into a man by magic and she throws
big men on the floor so they cry
and scratch their faces. Every morning
she tells her dreams. Now it has come,
what we were waiting for, we sit
on the sand, but there is no pond here.
I am ill and strange, my breasts are wet,
and everything is streaming out, streaming
into the sand and someone shouts and bleeds.

I watch. My sister puts her hands on me
to push me up, broken dolls, their faces eaten,
lie round, their faces thirsty, thirsty.
What do you have to pay to have
a sister or a brother? Like you pay
blood and milk for a baby, something
pours and pours out into the sand
and never stops, so you can hold
a hand and in the end you are not
someone else's, you are where
your sister lives, she is where you live,
you both are in the river washing the eaten faces.

Yellow Star

for Mother Maria Skobtsova

If we were true Christians, we would all wear the star
Mother Maria

Take down the star from the treetop:
after these two millennia, it is jaundiced,
scorched, its points still sharp enough, though,
to draw blood. When it first shone,
it lit the way to killing fields. It has not
lost its skill.

Pin the star with its glass spikes
over today's selected carriers
of the infections clouding the future's
blood. The star has made the rivers bitter,
bitter, the scorched neighbours cry out
with burnt tongues.

Pay for the star with forged certificates
of baptism, papers of citizenship securing
the right to emigrate from Christendom's
collapsing planet; hold up your hand
where the points have caught and drawn
polluting blood.

Step out, star child, into the queues
of neighbours lit by the lethal sign;
take bitter food and drink from the hand
of neighbours who pay the long price for being
there, always, under the light when we need
guilty strangers.

Hold up your hand; the star-drawn blood
binds you into the stranger's place.
While the light lasts, think how it is
that the dust of burned stars, the immeasurable
dust travels darkly over light years to reassemble,
alive and moist.

Please Close This Door Quietly

The slow, loud door: pushing against
a mound of dust, dust floating
heavily in a still room; step
slowly,

Stones can deceive. The ground looks
firm, but the dust makes you blink
and feel for purchase. This is
marshland,

Difficult light to sting eyes, terrain
whose spring and tangle hides deep
gaps, cold pools, old workings;
careful.

Too much left here of unseen lumber
dropped, knowingly or not, behind
the door to trip you while you rub
awkwardly

At naked eyes, opened on thick,
still, damp, scented air, imprinted,
used and recycled, not clearing up;
catching:

The weather of memory. Underfoot
lost tracks wind round an ankle
and abandoned diggings, wells, mines,
foundations,

Wait for your foot to find them,
drop you into the unexpected chill,
the snatched breath and swift
seeing,

The bird's flap at the edge
of your eye's world: things left
but alive; a space shared; a stone
yielding.

Alpine Morning (Bose)

Fine snow, swift at dawn; eyes closed,
then afterwards, the flakes
broad and slower.

Bird's foot touches the cold branch: snow
drops on snow. Silence
touching silence.

Line falls from the split web, a single
snowflake clings. Whispering
magnets.

Water far off drips in the unseen
rock bowl: sound of stars
in the dark.

The Spring, Blackden

Still. The hollow, green
and gold, and the flawless lip, promising
music.

The lip's note, level
frost, a ring to bind the falling water's
round blows.

Under the soil, humming,
lips closed till the frequencies break cover,
flower.

Shell Casing

Lying back broadly, arms flung out,
curling like feathers; the blood has dried
now, and it is quiet in the wet, ridged bed
where only minutes back voice, flesh,
air split so loudly open. Now
work is over, others must take it up,
connect the tubes, wash things away, arrange
for labelling the anonymous flesh.
Curling luxuriously upwards, a hollow dove,
the body waits to cuddle to itself
the scrap of a small cry, of a large
emptiness, inside the frozen wings,
below the broad smile on a face
absolved, unfocused, long past hearing.

Arabic Class in the Refugee Camp
(Islamabad 2006)

One by one the marks join up:
easing their way through the broken soil,
the green strands bend, twine,
dip and curl and cast off little drops
of rain. Nine months ago,
the soil broke up, shouting,
crushing its fist on houses, lives,
crops and futures, opening its wordless mouth
to say No. And the green strands
stubbornly grow back. The broken bits
of a lost harvest still let
the precious wires push through
to bind the pain, to join with knots and curls
the small hurt worlds of each
small life, to say another no: no,
you are not abandoned. The rope of words
is handed on, let down from a sky
broken by God's voice, curling and wrapping
each small life into the lines of grace,
the new world of the text that maps
our losses and our longings, so
that we can read humanity again
in one another's eyes, and hear
that the broken soil is not all, after all,
as the signs join up.

BaTwa in Boga

A wilting posy tied to his stick: heraldry,
like his plain shift, and the level of his face
more than a foot below us. How long
until we go home? Who knows we are here?
A few yards off his people have stopped
their buzz of not-quite-dancing.

We are dying here. Flies in a glass.
We are looked at here by the big folk;
who else knows? In the forest it is God
who looks at us. Out here he does not
see us, we do not see him. When
do we go home, out of the light
of your arrows?

There are, of course, says the UN man,
no pygmies in Boga. So no-one
is waiting to go home; and God in the forest
is content, of course.

Passion Plays

Gently the channels close. Businesslike as ever,
the flesh deals with the shaking spirit,
blood goes, resignedly, in search of different
pathways, and settles in unsightly pools on cheek
and throat, and the air vibrates embarrassingly
through stiffened pipes. The turbulence is kettled
in the hot plaza where the ribs bend in the dark,
trees bowed by wind at night.
                              Thumos, the Greeks said,
anger is what happens in your chest, when roads
up and down are blocked, and the noise
gets thinner and the blood builds up behind
the dams, the kettle shrieks and rattles
on its flame. You cannot sing in anger: only when
a steady drum settles the pulse, and the police
go home, when it is possible to walk, steadily,
around the square where arguments are sifted,
and the passion flows, now loud, now soft,
like notes, a word, an answer, beating a path
through black lanes where the walls ring
as the feet fall and the music ricochets.

Host Organism

I have been living
under the layers
of grain and moisture,
earth in my nostrils
and the years ahead
sitting like hard
pebbles in my gut,
and the hands that get
to sift the slack
grit while I sleep
fearfully through hours
of gardening labours,
pull themselves clear
and scrape nails clean
so that I feel the pricking
of green points that seek
pathways and waking
and tomorrow's work,
pushing out of the seed
dropped by some unnamed bird.

Hive

The empty garden fills. As you come
closer, the not quite silent wires,
the songlines, begin to weave. Walk
carefully: trip on the cords and who knows
what arrows might spring, what lethal
shocks arrest you, quivering, teeth
clamped, nerves flying. The tracks flow,
now, faster, into the drab house:
wait. There will be no invitation.
The log lines twine and crowd into the mouth
where the slow glistening boil
fills up the silence thickly. Somewhere
the messages are deposited, somewhere
the dust is brewed up into food and firelight.

Waters of Babylon

i.m. Joseph Brodsky

Tomi

One of them sat by the Black Sea,
his tongue dry from its stillness, afraid
that moisture on the buds would drown him
in a flood of tastes remembered, in a chaos
of pasts slipping from their triste moorings; afraid
of the toothbreaking dialects around him,
the grinning mouths flecked with food
he could not swallow. By the salt sea
he dried and slept; salted, hanging.

Babylon

And another, peeling the willow bark,
nails stained with green shreds, to plait
a basket, to place in it the eggshell-delicate
hopes of the day when they too will know
how a future can be extinguished, crushed like eggs,
the songs recorded for a grinning themepark,
he weaves away, nodding and smiling at his audience,
and the fast drops leak like a darting tongue
from the basket, green as a snake.

Venice/Ann Arbor/Hudson

And another, walking by the lagoons,
by the campus lakes, the river at the street's end,
his hunger is too fierce, his mouth overflows,
the chewed fragments scattering as he closes
teeth on words from the world's other side,
grinning and shameless, paid (he says) to wear out
the patience of the young, the solemn, the embarrassed:
he eats and eats until he cannot talk any more, ginger
hot in the mouth. And the moist muscles swell and burst.

Unsealings: School Play

for PW

Hand him a sealed envelope: a word
or number written inside to guess or maybe
see; the shape, like smoke, leaking out
to leave its smudges on the mind's sheet.

Tonight, though, it is not party tricks
for aspirant clairvoyants: you must hang out
your sheet against the wind of what my cold eye
expects to be consoling kitsch, singalong emotion.

Words handed to you; under the hot
light, what leaks out from inside the seals?
Shapes blossom into smoke, all that the words hide,
obsession, parents' guilt, loss, realism, all of the secrets

Stored up for you thirty years from now (please God),
drift from the page, smearing your sixteen-
summered eyes with smuts and grey water,
and I forget for a moment who you are,

Looking into the cloud of what you see,
what you are channelling, a hot mind steaming
the envelopes, baring skin to be scalded where
the dark thirty years ahead glances and spits,

All that you know, all that you cannot know,
your shadowed eyes and soot-flecked voice
parking authoritatively, for a few minutes,
the ready-made tricks, thrown without warning

into a foreign love, the accent of a feeling stranger.

Waldo Williams
Two Poems translated from the Welsh

What is Man?

What is living? The broad hall found
between narrow walls.
What is acknowledging? Finding the one root
under the branches' tangle.

What is believing? Watching at home
till the time arrives for welcome.
What is forgiving? Pushing your way through thorns
to stand alongside your old enemy.

What is singing? The ancient gifted breath
drawn in creating.
What is labour but making songs
From the wood and the wheat?

What is it to govern kingdoms? A skill
still crawling on all fours.
And arming kingdoms? A knife placed
in a baby's fist.

What is it to be a people? A gift
lodged in the heart's deep folds.
What is love of country? Keeping house
among a cloud of witnesses.

What is the world to the wealthy and strong? A wheel,
Turning and turning.
What is the world to earth's little ones? A cradle,
rocking and rocking.

Young Girl

That was what the stone carcase once was, a girl;
each time I see these bones, she takes hold of me again,
and back I go to her haunts, with every year of mine
answering for a century of hers.

She lived among people who knew what peace was,
buying their goods from the earth and the earth's gifts,
wondering silently at birth, marriage and death, tending
the human kindred's bonds.

All too soon she was put away, in her eternal foetus-crouch:
twelve times she greeted the arrival of May, and then
began to keep company with the darkness that took her, her voice
no longer heard on the hill.

So that the wide sky became deeper on account of her,
the blue sky brighter on account of her, and
the unseen ageless house above the hill's peaks more firmly founded
on account of her.

A child's skeleton in the Avebury museum, from around 2,500 BC.